100 ITIL® Foundation Exam Questions

Pass Your ITIL® Foundation Exam

for ITIL® v3 and ITIL® 2011

Brady Orand

PUBLISHED BY

ITILYaBrady

www.ITILYaBrady.com

Copyright © 2013 by Brady Orand

ISBN 1484167740

EAN-13 978-1484167748

Preface

Having taught IT Service Management courses for many years, I have seen first-hand the stress that an impending certification exam can have on students. For some, it has been many years since they have taken an exam so they are out of practice. Even years ago, the thought of taking an exam may have been very stressful.

This book is for all of those that need that little bit of extra help in preparing for, learning about, and finding your focus for the ITIL Foundation exam - whether you are preparing for v3 or ITIL 2011.

Writing a book is a significant undertaking. I've gone to great lengths to make sure that we provide the most current and most accurate information within these pages. However there's bound to be an error or two. If you find errors or would like to share your critique, please feel free to contact me. It is the feedback that I get from readers that helps me improve over time.

Brady Orand

Brady@ITILYaBrady.com

September 21, 2011

About the Author

I have been an ITIL® instructor since 2005. Even though I worked in the IT field for nearly two and a half decades, I did not truly understand IT until my first exposure to ITIL® three years earlier through my ITIL® Foundations course. Ever since then, I have been pursuing my ITIL® education to be the best instructor that I can be. Along this path, I have obtained many of the ITIL® v2 certifications, including the Service Manager certification, as well as all the certifications for ITIL® v3 (and now ITIL® 2011).

I started my corporate career as an intern at a microchip company you may have heard of, called Intel®. My job was to develop parts of a software product for Novell® networks. Even though this was the early 1990s, I still run across some people who continue use the products that I helped create.

I then went on to a company that focuses solely on software, BMC Software®, where I was responsible for a line of integration products that integrated BMC's products with other vendor products. This is where I really started learning the complexities of managing the IT infrastructure. This is also where I started my consulting and training career.

After BMC, my career led to a big-five consulting firm where I learned what "big projects" really are. As part of a 1,000-person project, I had the opportunity to learn more about the operational aspects of IT and how critical effective processes are to the success of such a large organization. I often look back on this experience and think about how we did things that were right, how we did things that were wrong and how both of these are addressed by ITIL®.

My first true teaching opportunity came when I then joined a smaller consulting company based outside of Chicago. As the ITIL® Practice Manager, my job was to create offerings around the concepts of IT Service Management®. The majority of my time was spent building training offerings and delivering this training. This is where I found that I truly enjoyed delivering training. However, the travel wasn't as much fun as it used to be.

I now work independently as a trainer, training course provider and consultant. I deliver training on behalf several companies, but the travel is much more tolerable. This also gives me the opportunity to pursue many of my own interests, such as study guides, exam preparation material, white papers, and other pursuits.

Contents

ABOUT THE EXAM

INTRODUCTION

This book is intended to assist you in your preparation for the ITIL® Foundation exam. This book does not replace the need for training - either formal classroom training or self-study.

The questions in this book come from a database of questions that I developed directly from the ITIL® syllabus published by the APM Group. Having taught ITIL® for many years, I have developed a sense of what types of questions may be asked and the format in which they may be presented. This book is intended to present you with questions that mimic the content, structure and format of your ITIL® Foundation exam.

More information, study resources, book updates and additional exam questions can be found on my website www.ITILyaBrady.com.

QUICK EXAM FACTS

Number of Questions: 40

Duration: 1 hour (those for whom the language is not in their native language can get an extra 15 minutes and the use of a dictionary)

Format: Multiple-choice

Reference Material: None

Passing Score: 65% (26 out of 40)

Exam Delivery: Paper-based or online

ABOUT THE EXAM

The exam itself is fairly straightforward. There are no "trick" questions, but many people have reported that the wording of the exam can be difficult. The more time you spend with sample exams of the same format, the more comfortable you will become with the wording.

The exam itself consists of 40 multiple-choice questions. Each question will be accompanied with four potential answers. There will be only one correct answer that you should choose. The four answers will be 'A,' 'B,' 'C,' or 'D'. Choose one and only one and do not leave any answers blank. In order to pass the exam, you need to get 26 out of 40 questions correct. While missing 14 questions may seem like a lot, it shows that the exam is not trivial.

The ITIL Foundations exam tests the candidate's knowledge regarding all aspect of the service lifecycle, general concepts, and select processes and functions within the service lifecycle. This requires a broad understanding of the service lifecycle. The ITIL Foundation syllabus outlines each of the required knowledge areas to be successful on the exam. Of the 40 questions on the ITIL Foundations exam, the general distribution is from the following topic areas:

Service Management as a Practice	3 questions
The ITIL Service Lifecycle	5 questions
Generic Concepts and Definitions	6 questions
Key Principles and Model	4 questions
Processes	18 questions
Functions	2 questions
Roles	1 question
Technology and Architecture	1 question

QUESTION FORMAT

The questions themselves can differ dramatically in the format but typically fall into a few general formats.

Basic Format

The basic format questions are of the form of question and four answers:

1. What color is an apple?

    A. Blue
    B. Purple
    C. Red
    D. Pink

These questions are the simplest and are looking for the basic answer. While it may be possible to identify more than one answer under special circumstances ("I can think of a time when I have seen a blue apple"), the examiners are looking for the answer that best suits what you learned in your ITIL Foundations course.

Basic Negative Format

The basic negative format question is opposite the basic format question and looks for the answer that is not true about the topic. This format looks like this:

1. Apples can be all of the following colors EXCEPT:

    A. Green
    B. Red
    C. Blue
    D. Yellow

These questions can be a little more difficult. The approach that I employ is to look at each answer independently and determine if that answer is consistent with the concepts within ITIL. The answer that is not consistent is the answer that is correct for the question being asked.

Multiple-Part Format

Another type of challenging question that comes up is the multiple-part questions. While there are only 40 questions on the exam, this is one way the examiners can ask more than 40 questions. The format of these questions look like this:

2. Which of the following statements about apples are correct?

    1. Apples grow on trees

    2. Apples are citrus

    3. Apples are roundish in shape

    4. Apples can be used in pie filling

    A. 1, 2 and 3 only
    B. 2 and 4 only
    C. 1, 3 and 4 only
    D. All of the above

My approach to these types of questions is to ask myself multiple questions ("Do apples grow on trees?", "Are apples citrus?", etc.) and identify the answer that is consistent with what I came up with. However, I also look at the other answers to check myself and ensure that I didn't miss anything.

On these types of questions, you may only be able to identify a part of it that you know to be true and not be sure about the other parts. When this happens, find the answer(s) that are consistent with your knowledge and eliminate the other answer(s). This allows you to focus on the candidate answers and not be distracted.

Note that on these types of questions, you may find that all of the statements are true or none of them are true. Candidate answers could be "All of the above" or "None of the above".

Other Exam Tips

There are many ways to ask questions about the same topic. You will experience this in the questions on the following pages. Because of this, read the question carefully! Do not assume that because the first few words are just like a sample question from a mock exam, or from this book, that the exact same question is being asked.

Additionally, read the answers carefully. You may see a question just like one on a mock exam, but the answers may be very different. This is not a memorization exam, but one that tests your knowledge of the subject matter.

About the Following Questions

The questions in the pages that follow come from a database of questions that I developed. I developed these questions by going through the syllabus line by line and identifying potential basic questions, negative questions and multiple-part questions that I would ask if I were writing the exam. I also reviewed the types of questions that are found on the official mock exam with regard to content and format. The toughest part about creating these exam questions was not the question, but the incorrect answers. It is my belief that many of the questions on the following pages are tougher than many that you will find on the real exam, but this should work out to your benefit.

Additional exam questions and the official mock exams can be found on my website www.ITILYaBrady.com for your benefit.

On to the questions!

100 Exam Questions

In the pages that follow are one hundred sample exam questions. These exam questions represent the types of questions that you will see on the ITIL® Foundations exam.

Of the 40 questions on the ITIL® Foundations exam, the distribution is from the following topics:

Service Management as a Practice	3 questions
The ITIL® Service Lifecycle	5 questions
Generic Concepts and Definitions	6 questions
Key Principles and Model	4 questions
Processes	18 questions
Functions	2 questions
Roles	1 question
Technology and Architecture	1 question

The questions in the pages that follow have the same distribution from the various topic areas for the ITIL® Foundation exam.

1. The ability of a service to meet appropriate levels of availability, capacity, continuity and security refers to what?

    A. Fit for purpose

    B. Warranty

    C. Value

    D. Functionality

2. A set of documents that included everything necessary for the build, test, implementation and operation of a service is known as which of the following?

    A. Service Design Package

    B. Service Requirements

    C. Service Transition Package

    D. Service Strategy

3. To what does the phrase "the underlying cause of one or more incidents" refer?

    A. Problem

    B. Workaround

    C. Error

    D. Fault

4. Reducing or eliminating the impact of an incident or problem for which a full resolution is not yet available is a description of which of the following terms?

    A. Workaround

    B. Resolution

    C. Incident

    D. Problem

5. Which of the following might a stakeholder be interested in?

    1. Activities of a project

    2. Deliverables from service management

    3. Targets of a project

        A. None of the above

        B. 1 and 2 only

        C. 2 and 3 only

        D. All of the above

6. A function can best be described as what?

    A. The specific activity within a process

    B. The people and the tools they use that perform the activities of one or more processes

    C. The delivery of service solutions to the customers to enable business outcomes

    D. None of the above

7. Which role is responsible for carrying out one or more process activities?

    A. Process manager

    B. Process practitioner

    C. Process owner

    D. Process functions

8. What term refers to "those who use the service on a day-to-day basis?"

    A. Users

    B. Customers

    C. Suppliers

    D. People

9. In which stage of the service lifecycle is it determined what services are provided and to whom they are provided?

    A.   Service Strategy

    B.   Service Design

    C.   Continual Service Improvement

    D.   Service Operation

10. The service portfolio defines services in terms of what?

    A.   Business outcomes

    B.   Provider outcomes

    C.   Resources and capabilities

    D.   Value

11. Warranty is the assurance that a service is fit for use. How else can warranty be expressed?

    A.   Any means by which the service provider supports the service

    B.   Any means by which the service is supported by an external third party guarantee

    C.   Any means by which an organization that supports a service is defined

    D.   Any means by which utility is made available to users

12. Which of the following are the two categories of activities to address risk?

    1. Risk analysis

    2. Risk mitigation

    3. Risk management

        A.   1 and 2

        B.   2 and 3

        C.   1 and 3

        D.   None of the above

13. Value of a service is provided through what two components?

    A. Processes and functions

    B. Risks and costs

    C. Utility and warranty

    D. Resources and capabilities

14. A Service Level Agreement (SLA) for a single customer for all services for that customer is called what?

    A. Customer-based SLA

    B. Operational Level Agreement (OLA)

    C. Service-based SLA

    D. Customer catalog

15. The set of tools and databases used to store a service provider's configuration information is called what?

    A. Configuration Management System

    B. Configuration Management Database

    C. Service Knowledge Management System

    D. Availability Management Information System

16. Which of the core ITIL publications are intended for only external service providers?

    A. Service Strategy

    B. Service Transition

    C. All except Service Strategy

    D. None of the above

17. To which of the following does the phrase "the addition, modification or removal of anything that could have an effect on IT services" refer?

    A. Change

    B. Request for Change

    C. Change Management

    D. Service Change

18. What are the reasons that ITIL has been successful?

    1. ITIL is vendor-neutral

    2. ITIL is non-prescriptive

    3. ITIL represents best practice

      A. 3 only

      B. 1 and 2 only

      C. All of the above

      D. None of the above

19. What is a problem model?

    A. A way to resolve an incident in a standardized way

    B. A set of predefined steps to take when dealing with a particular type of problem

    C. A graphical representation of the cause of a problem

    D. A way to resolve all problems easily

20. Which of the following is the best description of a change model?

    A. A set of predefined steps to be followed when dealing with a known type of change

    B. A pre-approval of changes so they do not have to be evaluated by the CAB

    C. A mechanism to evaluate all changes to ensure no impact to the production environment

    D. A standard deployment technique

21. Which of the following activities would be expected of a process owner?

    1. Defining the process strategy

    2. Ensuring that activities are carried out

    3. Creating or updating records to show that activities have been carried out effectively

      A. All of the above

      B. 2 and 3 only

      C. 1 only

      D. 1 and 3 only

22. What is the primary measure of Business Relationship Management?

     A.   Customer satisfaction

     B.   Number of services provided to the customer

     C.   Achieving agreed levels of service

     D.   All of the above

23. Which of the following is not a part of the service portfolio?

     A.   Service pipeline

     B.   Service definition

     C.   Service catalog

     D.   Retired services

24. Which of the following are included in the five major aspects of design?

        1. Service solution itself

        2. Service operation process designs to support a new or changed service

        3. Technical architectures

        4. Environmental architectures

        5. Service Portfolio

             A.   1 and 2 only

             B.   2, 3 and 4 only

             C.   None of these are included in the five major aspects of design

             D.   All of the above

25. Which of the following cannot be stored in a tool or a database?

     A.   Data

     B.   Information

     C.   Knowledge

     D.   Wisdom

26. Which of the following would be the best candidate for a service request?

    A. Request for a change to a global security profile

    B. Request for a contract review with the vendor

    C. Request for a resolution to a failure in a component of a service

    D. Request for a toner cartridge for a desktop printer

27. In which part of the service portfolio are details of all operational services recorded?

    A. Service pipeline

    B. Service catalog

    C. Retired services

    D. None of the above

28. What the service does, refers to what?

    A. Warranty

    B. Utility

    C. Enabling service

    D. Value

29. Which Service Operation process is responsible for dealing with requests from users?

    A. Request Fulfillment

    B. Incident Management

    C. Service Desk

    D. Access Management

30. What are three types of change according to ITIL?

    A. Change, service change, modification

    B. Standard change, normal change, emergency change

    C. User change, IT change, business change

    D. Minor change, major change, urgent change

31. Which of the following is the best description of the Service Desk function?

    A. The single point of contact for all operational issues from users

    B. The single point of contact for all business changes

    C. The single point of contact for vendors to submit incidents

    D. The single point of contact between customers and IT

32. To which of the following does the term service metric refer?

    A. The end-to-end measurement of a service

    B. The measurement of customer satisfaction

    C. The response time at the Service Desk

    D. The measurement of the underlying processes that support the service

33. Which of the following is not a classification of a service?

    A. External service

    B. Core service

    C. Enabling service

    D. Enhancing service

34. For what is Application Management not responsible?

    A. Developing code required for applications

    B. Supporting applications

    C. Assisting with the design, testing and deployment of applications

    D. All of the above

35. Providing a consistent and single source of information for all services that are in operation or are prepared to be run operationally is the responsibility of which process?

    A. Service Strategy

    B. Service Level Management

    C. Service Catalog Management

    D. Service Operation

36. To what does the statement "ensures that policies and strategy are actually implemented, and that required processes are correctly followed" refer?

    A. Assurance

    B. Governance

    C. Strategy

    D. Audit

37. The measure of how long a service, component or CI can perform its agreed function without interruption refers to which of the following terms?

    A. Availability

    B. Reliability

    C. Maintainability

    D. Serviceability

38. What is a Configuration Item (CI)?

    A. Business assets that support critical business processes

    B. Anything necessary in the delivery of technical services

    C. Any asset of an organization

    D. Anything that is under the control of Configuration Management

39. Which of the following does service automation improve?

    A. Capabilities and resources

    B. Functions and processes

    C. Utility and warranty

    D. Value and cost

40. What is the purpose of IT Service Continuity Management?

    A. To support the overall Business Continuity Management process

    B. To monitor the availability of business processes

    C. To provide for disaster recovery of IT services

    D. To deliver plans for IT to support the business

41. What are the three types of metrics as defined within CSI?

    A.   Process, technology, service

    B.   Program, Project and Personnel

    C.   Organization, Business, Customer

    D.   Baseline, benchmark, audit

42. In which stage of the service lifecycle include Service Catalog Managmeent, Supplier Management and Information Security Management?

    A.   Service Strategy

    B.   Service Design

    C.   Service Transition

    D.   Service Operation

43. Which Service Operation function is responsible to be the custodian of information regarding the infrastructure?

    A.   Application Management

    B.   Facilities Management

    C.   Configuration Management

    D.   Technical Management

44. Services facilitate what?

    A.   Risks

    B.   Revenue

    C.   Outcomes

    D.   Costs

45. To what does the term 'rights' refer?

    A.   The permissions granted to a user or role

    B.   Information about a user that distinguishes one individual user from another

    C.   The level or extent of a service's functionality that a user is entitled to

    D.   None of the above

46. Which of the following is the best description of IT Service Management?

    A. A means of delivering value to customers by facilitating outcomes customers want to achieve without the ownership of costs and risks

    B. The implementation and management of quality IT services that meet the needs of the business

    C. Both of the above

    D. None of the above

47. The main output of Service Operation is which of the following?

    A. Tested services to Continual Service Improvement

    B. Service Performance Reports to Service Design

    C. Service Operations Package to Service Transition

    D. Service Performance Reports to Continual Service Improvement

48. What is a customer-based Service Level Agreement (SLA)?

    A. An SLA between customers

    B. An SLA for a single customer for all services for that customer

    C. An SLA for a single service applicable to all customers of that service

    D. None of the above

49. The two sub-functions of IT Operation Management are which of the following?

    A. Request Management and Data Center Management

    B. Application Management and Technical Management

    C. Operations Control and Facilities Management

    D. Facilities Management and Request Management

50. To what does the term 'stakeholder' refer?

    A.   The customers who fund the service

    B.   The users who use a service

    C.   Anyone with an interest in an organization, project, service, etc.

    D.   The people performing the activities within a process

51. What would be the next step in the Continual Service Improvement Model / Approach after

    1. What is the vision?

    2. Where are we now?

    3. Where do we want to be?

    4. How do we get there?

    5. Did we get there?

        A.   How much did it cost?

        B.   How do we keep the momentum going?

        C.   What was the value on investment?

        D.   What is the Total Cost of Ownership (TCO)?

52. Which stage of the service lifecycle is responsible for the design of new and changed services?

    A.   Service Level Management

    B.   Service Transition

    C.   Service Strategy

    D.   Service Design

53. The purpose of Access Management is what?

    A.   To define security policies to be followed

    B.   To provide the right for users to be able to use a service or group of services

    C.   To audit security throughout the service provider organization

    D.   To ensure that access to services is available to all who ask

54. Which of the following is not a value to business of the Service Strategy stage of the service lifecycle?

    A. Effectively design new and changed services

    B. Enable an understanding of what types and levels of services make its customer successful

    C. Enable the activities performed by the service provider to be linked to business outcomes enabling the service provider to be seen as contributing to the value of the business

    D. Facilitate functional and transparent communications between the customer and the service provider so that both have a consistent understanding of what is required and how it will be delivered

55. Which of the following statements regarding Patterns of Business Activity is not correct?

    A. They are dynamic over time

    B. They represent the dynamics of the business

    C. They are impossible to forecast

    D. They should be documented and be an input to capacity management to plan capacity

56. Which of the following activities is carried out in the "Where do we want to be" step of the continual service improvement model?

    A. Aligning the business and IT strategies

    B. Implementing service and process improvements

    C. Creating a baseline

    D. Defining measurable targets

57. Management, organization, processes and knowledge refer to what type of service asset?

    A. Functions

    B. Outcome support

    C. Resources

    D. Capabilities

58. Which of the following statements regarding Problem Management are correct?

      1. When resolutions to problems require a change, they do not have to go through Change Management.

      2. Problem Management stores information about the underlying errors and workarounds in the Known Error Database (KEDB).

      3. Problem categorization and incident categorization are most likely to be identical.

      4. Problem Management activities are entirely reactive.

        A.   1, 3 and 4

        B.   2 only

        C.   4 only

        D.   2 and 3 only

59. What is a service-based Service Level Agreement (SLA)?

    A.   An SLA between service providers

    B.   An SLA for a single customer for all services for that customer

    C.   An SLA for a single service applicable to all customers of that service

    D.   An SLA between two parts of the same organization

60. What Service Operation process is responsible for managing the lifecycle of all service requests from the users?

    A.   Request Fulfillment

    B.   Request Management

    C.   Service Desk

    D.   Incident Management

61. Which of the following is Supplier Management responsible for?

    A.   Operational Level Agreements (OLA)

    B.   Underpinning contracts (UC)

    C.   Service Level Requirements (SLR)

    D.   Service Level Agreements (SLA)

62. What is the name of the set of documents that serves as the main output of Service Design into Service Transition?

    A.   Service Transition Package (STP)

    B.   Service Operation Package (SOP)

    C.   Service Design Package (SDP)

    D.   Service Level Package (SLP)

63. Which of the following characteristics do not contribute to the success of ITIL?

    A.   ITIL is vendor-neutral

    B.   ITIL is non-prescriptive

    C.   ITIL is totally independent of any other standard, methodology or framework

    D.   ITIL represents best practice

64. Which of the following is the best definition of a risk?

    A.   A possible event that could cause harm or loss

    B.   The discontinuation of a project

    C.   The potential reorganization of the service provider

    D.   The analysis of things that might happen to affect the service

65. Which of the following is the best description of reliability?

 A. The ability of a service, component or CI to perform its agreed function when required

 B. A measure of how long a service, component or CI can perform its agreed function without interruption

 C. A measure of how quickly and effectively a service, component or CI can be restored to normal working after a failure

 D. The ability of a third-party supplier to meet the terms of its contract

66. A notification that a threshold has been violated is called what?

 A. Event

 B. Warning

 C. Alert

 D. Incident

67. What are the first four steps of the CSI Model / CSI Approach?

 A. Identify measurable targets, understand the vision, outline the plan for improvement, assess the current environment

 B. Understand the vision, assess the current environment, identify measurable targets, outline a plan for improvement

 C. Assess the current environment, understand the vision, identify measurable targets, outline the plan for improvement

 D. Outline the plan for improvement, understand the vision, assess the current environment, identify measurable targets

68. What is an underpinning contract (UC)?

  A. An agreement between two parts of the same organization

  B. An agreement between and IT service provider and an external third party

  C. A requirement for a specific aspect of an IT service

  D. An agreement between IT and their customer

69. What is an Operational Level Agreement (OLA)?

  A. An agreement between two parts of the same organization

  B. An agreement between and IT service provider and an external third party

  C. A requirement for a specific aspect of an IT service

  D. An agreement between IT and their customer

70. To what does the phrase "those who buy goods or services" refer?

  A. Customers

  B. Users

  C. Service providers

  D. Suppliers

71. Which of the following is not a type of event?

  A. Informational

  B. Warning

  C. Exception

  D. Alert

72. Incident prioritization is determined by what?

  A. Time and complexity

  B. Resources and capabilities

  C. Complexity and resources

  D. Urgency and impact

73. Capabilities are which of the following:

    A. The intangible elements of a service asset

    B. The tangible elements of a service asset

    C. The money the service asset requires to procure it

    D. The value the service provider delivers to the business

74. To what does the phrase "any change of state that has significance for the management of a service" refer?

    A. Event

    B. Alert

    C. Change

    D. Service request

75. What is the last step in the CSI Model / CSI Approach?

    A. Establish a baseline

    B. Identify further opportunities for improvement

    C. Understand the vision for improvement

    D. Outline the plans for improvement

76. Service metrics measure which of the following?

    A. Underlying components that support services

    B. Customer service statistics

    C. End-to-end service

    D. Resources and capabilities

77. A measure of how quickly and effectively a service, component or CI can be restored to normal working after a failure refers to which of the following terms?

    A. Availability

    B. Reliability

    C. Maintainability

    D. Serviceability

78. Complementary guidance refers to what?

    A. The free process maps that are included as available download

    B. The service that ITIL provides to assess a service provider's process maturity

    C. The industry that has been created around the service management profession

    D. Additional publications providing guidance specific to industry sectors, organization types, operating models and technology architectures

79. Which of the following is the best description of a standard change?

    A. A pre-authorized change with an accepted and established procedure

    B. A change to the organizational policies and standards

    C. A checklist for changes

    D. A change that does not require following the Change Management process

80. Which process is responsible for the negotiation of underpinning contracts?

    A. Service Catalog Management

    B. Supplier Management

    C. Service Level Management

    D. Contract Management

81. Which of the following is not an advantage provided by service automation?

    A. Increased consistency in reporting

    B. Easier adjustment of workload to meet capacity demands

    C. Improved consistency of service

    D. Improved organizational structure

82. Which of the following statements regarding Business Relationship Management (BRM) and Service Level Management (SLM) is/are correct?

    1. BRM focuses on user satisfaction

    2. SLM focuses on strategic relationships

    3. SLM focuses on delivering specific levels of service to the business

    4. BRM focuses on delivering long-term customer satisfaction

        A. None of the above

        B. 1, 2 and 3 only

        C. 3 and 4 only

        D. All of the above

83. Which of the following would not be stored in the DML?

    A. Change schedule for a business service

    B. Video files as part of a service

    C. Desktop images for standard desktop configurations

    D. Application release candidates from the application development team

84. Which Service Design process performs service reviews with the customer on a regular basis?

    A. Service Operation

    B. Service Catalog Management

    C. Service Level Management

    D. Service Reporting

85. Order the following Continual Service Improvement (CSI) implementation steps into the correct sequence in alignment with the Plan, Do, Check, Act (PDCA) model

    1. Allocate roles and responsibilities to work on CSI initiatives

    2. Measure and review that the CSI plan is executed and its objectives are being achieved

    3. Identify the scope, objectives and requirements for CSI

    4. Implement CSI enhancement

        A. 3-1-2-4

        B. 4-3-1-2

        C. 2-3-1-4

        D. 2-1-4-3

86. Which of the following is not a function within Service Operation?

    A. Application Management

    B. Technical Management

    C. Facilities Management

    D. Request Fulfillment

87. Which of the following statements about Configuration Items (CIs) is/are true?

    1. Configuration Management monitors the performance characteristics of every CI

    2. CIs have attributes in which to record information about that CI or CI type

        A. 1 only

        B. 2 only

        C. 1 and 2

        D. Neither statement is correct

88. Which model provides a view of the services, assets and infrastructure and their relationships to each other?

    A.   Change Model

    B.   Incident Model

    C.   Configuration Model

    D.   Request Model

89. The service lifecycle refers to all stages in the life of an IT service and includes the stages of Service Operation, Continual Service Improvement, Service Design and what other stage(s)?

    1. Service Optimization

    2. Service Definition

    3. Service Transition

    4. Service Outcomes

    5. Service Strategy

        A.   1 and 2 only

        B.   2, 3 and 5 only

        C.   3 and 5 only

        D.   2, 3, 4 and 5 only

90. What is the relationship between metrics and Key Performance Indicators (KPIs)?

    A.   All metrics are KPIs

    B.   They are the same thing

    C.   KPIs are the most important metrics that support CSFs

    D.   They are unrelated

91. What is referred to by the phrase "represents the commitments and investments made by a service provider across all customers and market spaces?"

    A.   Service Strategy

    B.   Service Portfolio

    C.   Service Investment

    D.   Service Value

92. Which of the following techniques is most often used to assess risks to the business due to loss of IT service?

    A.   Knowledge transfer

    B.   RACI Model

    C.   Component Failure Impact Analysis (CFIA)

    D.   Business Impact Analysis (BIA)

93. What is the first step in the CSI Model / CSI Approach?

    A.   What is the vision?

    B.   Where are we now?

    C.   How do we get there?

    D.   How do we keep the momentum going?

94. Which stage of the Service Lifecycle includes the processes of Availability Management and Supplier Management?

    A.   Service Strategy

    B.   Service Design

    C.   Service Transition

    D.   Service Operation

95. Which of the following responsibilities would be expected of a service owner?

    A.   Defining the process strategy

    B.   Carrying out the activities of a process

    C.   Representing the service across the organization

    D.   Implementing changes to a service

96. What should the CSI register be part of?

    A.   CMS

    B.   SKMS

    C.   KEDB

    D.   DIKW Model

97. Identifying ways to improve processes, services and become more cost effective is part of which stage of the service lifecycle?

    A. Service Transition

    B. Service Strategy

    C. Service Operation

    D. Continual Service Improvement

98. Which of the following would be the best example of an enabling service?

    A. Shipping service that supports the business outcome of shipping products in a timely manner.

    B. Network service that supports communication between components

    C. Service Desk

    D. None of the above

99. In which stage of the service lifecycle are the functional requirements documented and service levels agreed?

    A. Service Strategy

    B. Service Transition

    C. Service Design

    D. Service Operation

100. What is an alert?

    A. A notification that a threshold has been violated

    B. An occurrence that is significant for the management of a service

    C. An audible notification

    D. An emergency meeting to evaluate a change

ANSWERS AND RATIONALES

Q#		Q#		Q#		Q#		Q#	
1	B	21	C	41	A	61	B	81	D
2	A	22	A	42	B	62	C	82	C
3	A	23	B	43	D	63	C	83	A
4	A	24	D	44	C	64	A	84	C
5	D	25	D	45	A	65	B	85	A
6	B	26	D	46	B	66	C	86	D
7	B	27	B	47	D	67	B	87	B
8	A	28	B	48	B	68	B	88	C
9	A	29	A	49	C	69	A	89	C
10	D	30	B	50	C	70	A	90	C
11	D	31	A	51	B	71	D	91	B
12	A	32	A	52	D	72	D	92	D
13	C	33	A	53	B	73	A	93	A
14	A	34	A	54	A	74	A	94	B
15	A	35	C	55	C	75	B	95	C
16	D	36	B	56	D	76	C	96	B
17	A	37	B	57	D	77	C	97	D
18	C	38	D	58	D	78	D	98	B
19	B	39	C	59	C	79	A	99	C
20	A	40	A	60	A	80	B	100	A

1. The ability of a service to meet appropriate levels of availability, capacity, continuity and security refers to what?

    A. Fit for purpose

    B. Warranty

    C. Value

    D. Functionality

    Warranty is the assurance that product or service will meet its agreed requirement and is provided through appropriate levels of availability, capacity, continuity and security.

    Question ID: 47 / Topic: Generic Concepts and Definitions

2. A set of documents that included everything necessary for the build, test, implementation and operation of a service is known as which of the following?

    A. Service Design Package

    B. Service Requirements

    C. Service Transition Package

    D. Service Strategy

    The Service Design Package (SDP) defines all aspects of an IT service and its requirements through each stage of its lifecycle.

    Question ID: 214 / Topic: Generic Concepts and Definitions

3. To what does the phrase "the underlying cause of one or more incidents" refer?

    A. Problem

    B. Workaround

    C. Error

    D. Fault

    A problem is defined as the underlying cause of one or more incidents.

    Question ID: 141 / Topic: Service Operation Major Processes

4. Reducing or eliminating the impact of an incident or problem for which a full resolution is not yet available is a description of which of the following terms?

   A. Workaround

   B. Resolution

   C. Incident

   D. Problem

A workaround is defined as reducing or eliminating the impact of an incident or problem for which a full resolution is not yet available.

Question ID: 194 / Topic: Service Operation Major Processes

5. Which of the following might a stakeholder be interested in?

   1. Activities of a project

   2. Deliverables from service management

   3. Targets of a project

      A. None of the above

      B. 1 and 2 only

      C. 2 and 3 only

      D. All of the above

Stakeholders have an interest in an organization, project or service etc, and may be interested in the activities, targets, resources or deliverables from service management.

Question ID: 41 / Topic: Service Management as a Practice

6. A function can best be described as what?

   A. The specific activity within a process

   B. The people and the tools they use that perform the activities of one or more processes

   C. The delivery of service solutions to the customers to enable business outcomes

   D. None of the above

A function is defined as the team or group of people and the tools they use to carry out the activities of one or more processes.

Question ID: 55 / Topic: Service Management as a Practice

7. Which role is responsible for carrying out one or more process activities?

    A.   Process manager

    B.   Process practitioner

    C.   Process owner

    D.   Process functions

The process owner defines the process strategy.

The process manager ensures that activities are carried out.

The process practitioner is responsible for carrying out one or more process activities.

Question ID: 23 / Topic: Roles

8. What term refers to "those who use the service on a day-to-day basis?"

    A.   Users

    B.   Customers

    C.   Suppliers

    D.   People

Users are defined as those who use the service on a day-to-day basis.

Question ID: 102 / Topic: Generic Concepts and Definitions

9. In which stage of the service lifecycle is it determined what services are provided and to whom they are provided?

    A.   Service Strategy

    B.   Service Design

    C.   Continual Service Improvement

    D.   Service Operation

The purpose of the service strategy stage of the service lifecycle is to define the perspective, position, plans and patterns that a service provider needs to be able to execute to meet an organization's business outcomes. This translates to understanding who the customers are, their business needs, and how those needs an be met through services.

Question ID: 71 / Topic: The ITIL Service Lifecycle

10. The service portfolio defines services in terms of what?

    A.   Business outcomes

    B.   Provider outcomes

    C.   Resources and capabilities

    D.   Value

The service portfolio defines services in terms of the **value** the service provides. Not all services are directly related to the business (such as enabling services), so not all services provide business outcomes.

Question ID: 87 / Topic: Service Strategy Minor Processes

11. Warranty is the assurance that a service is fit for use. How else can warranty be expressed?

    A.   Any means by which the service provider supports the service

    B.   Any means by which the service is supported by an external third party guarantee

    C.   Any means by which an organization that supports a service is defined

    D.   Any means by which utility is made available to users

Warranty refers to the availability, capacity, continuity and security of a service and involves any means by which the utility of a service is made available to users.

Question ID: 49 / Topic: Generic Concepts and Definitions

12. Which of the following are the two categories of activities to address risk?

    1. Risk analysis

    2. Risk mitigation

    3. Risk management

      A.   ***1 and 2***

      B.   2 and 3

      C.   1 and 3

      D.   None of the above

Risk analysis and risk management are the two main activity categories to manage risk. Risk mitigation would be an activity within risk management.

Question ID: 97 / Topic: Generic Concepts and Definitions

13. Value of a service is provided through what two components?

      A.   Processes and functions

      B.   Risks and costs

      C.   ***Utility and warranty***

      D.   Resources and capabilities

The value of a service is provided through utility (what the service does) and warranty (assurance that it is fit for use).

Question ID: 46 / Topic: Generic Concepts and Definitions

14. A Service Level Agreement (SLA) for a single customer for all services for that customer is called what?

      A.   ***Customer-based SLA***

      B.   Operational Level Agreement (OLA)

      C.   Service-based SLA

      D.   Customer catalog

A service-based SLA is an SLA for a single service applicable to all customers of that service.

A customer-based SLA is an SLA for a single customer for all services for that customer.

Question ID: 232 / Topic: Service Design Major Processes

15. The set of tools and databases used to store a service provider's configuration information is called what?

    A. ***Configuration Management System***

    B. Configuration Management Database

    C. Service Knowledge Management System

    D. Availability Management Information System

    The Configuration Management System (CMS) is the set of tools and databases used to store a service providers configuration information.

    Question ID: 267 / Topic: Service Transition Minor Processes

16. Which of the core ITIL publications are intended for only external service providers?

    A. Service Strategy

    B. Service Transition

    C. All except Service Strategy

    D. ***None of the above***

    All of the guidance in the ITIL core publications are intended for both internal and external service providers.

    Question ID: 69 / Topic: The ITIL Service Lifecycle

17. To which of the following does the phrase "the addition, modification or removal of anything that could have an effect on IT services" refer?

    A. ***Change***

    B. Request for Change

    C. Change Management

    D. Service Change

    A change is defined as the addition, modification or removal of anything that could have an effect on IT services. A change is a broad scope that includes any modification.

    A service change is defined as the addition, modification or removal of an authorized, planned or supported service or service component and its associated documentation.

    Question ID: 166 / Topic: Service Transition Major Processes

18. What are the reasons that ITIL has been successful?

   1. ITIL is vendor-neutral

   2. ITIL is non-prescriptive

   3. ITIL represents best practice

   A. 3 only

   B. 1 and 2 only

   C. ***All of the above***

   D. None of the above

ITIL has achieved success because it is vendor-neutral, non-prescriptive, and represents the best practice learning experiences of best-in-class service providers.

Question ID: 25 / Topic: Service Management as a Practice

19. What is a problem model?

   A. A way to resolve an incident in a standardized way

   B. ***A set of predefined steps to take when dealing with a particular type of problem***

   C. A graphical representation of the cause of a problem

   D. A way to resolve all problems easily

A problem model is a set of predefined steps to take when dealing with a known type of problem. A problem model should include:

- The steps to take
- The chronological order to take these steps
- Responsibilities
- Timescales and thresholds
- Escalation procedures

Question ID: 131 / Topic: Service Operation Major Processes

20. Which of the following is the best description of a change model?

    A. A set of predefined steps to be followed when dealing with a known type of change

    B. A pre-approval of changes so they do not have to be evaluated by the CAB

    C. A mechanism to evaluate all changes to ensure no impact to the production environment

    D. A standard deployment technique

A change model is a set of predefined steps to be followed when dealing with a known type of change.

Question ID: 286 / Topic: Service Transition Major Processes

21. Which of the following activities would be expected of a process owner?

    1. Defining the process strategy

    2. Ensuring that activities are carried out

    3. Creating or updating records to show that activities have been carried out effectively

    A. All of the above

    B. 2 and 3 only

    C. 1 only

    D. 1 and 3 only

The process owner defines the process strategy.

The process manager ensures that activities are carried out.

The process practitioner creates or updates records to show that activities have been carried out effectively.

Question ID: 19 / Topic: Roles

22. What is the primary measure of Business Relationship Management?

    A. **Customer satisfaction**
    B. Number of services provided to the customer
    C. Achieving agreed levels of service
    D. All of the above

Customer satisfaction is the primary measure of Business Relationship Management. Achieving agreed levels of service is the primary measure of Service Level Management.

Question ID: 116 / Topic: Service Strategy Minor Processes

23. Which of the following is not a part of the service portfolio?

    A. Service pipeline
    B. **Service definition**
    C. Service catalog
    D. Retired services

The service portfolio contains the service pipeline, service catalog, and retired services.

Question ID: 88 / Topic: Service Strategy Minor Processes

24.   Which of the following are included in the five major aspects of design?

       1. Service solution itself

       2. Service operation process designs to support a new or changed service

       3. Technical architectures

       4. Environmental architectures

       5. Service Portfolio

          A.   1 and 2 only

          B.   2, 3 and 4 only

          C.   None of these are included in the five major aspects of design

          D.   All of the above

The five major aspects of design are STAMP:

- Service solution
- Tools and technology (such as the service portfolio)
- Architectures
- Measurements and metrics
- Processes

Question ID: 220 / Topic: Key Principles and Models

25.   Which of the following cannot be stored in a tool or a database?

       A.   Data

       B.   Information

       C.   Knowledge

       D.   Wisdom

Wisdom cannot be stored in a database or a tool.

Question ID: 294 / Topic: Service Transition Minor Processes

26. Which of the following would be the best candidate for a service request?

   A. Request for a change to a global security profile

   B. Request for a contract review with the vendor

   C. Request for a resolution to a failure in a component of a service

   D. *Request for a toner cartridge for a desktop printer*

   A service request is a description for many different types of demands that are placed on IT by the users. Service Requests are generally requests for information, a standard change, access to a service or a consumable such as a toner cartridge.

   Question ID: 137 / Topic: Service Operation Minor Processes

27. In which part of the service portfolio are details of all operational services recorded?

   A. Service pipeline

   B. *Service catalog*

   C. Retired services

   D. None of the above

   Details of all operational services are recorded within the service catalog.

   Question ID: 89 / Topic: Service Strategy Minor Processes

28. What the service does, refers to what?

   A. Warranty

   B. *Utility*

   C. Enabling service

   D. Value

   Utility is the functionality offered by a product or service and refers to 'what the service does'.

   Question ID: 45 / Topic: Generic Concepts and Definitions

29. Which Service Operation process is responsible for dealing with requests from users?

   A.   Request Fulfillment

   B.   Incident Management

   C.   Service Desk

   D.   Access Management

A service request is a description for many different types of demands that are placed on IT by the users. Service Requests are generally requests for information, a standard change, access to a service or a consumable such as a toner cartridge.

Question ID: 139 / Topic: Service Operation Minor Processes

30. What are three types of change according to ITIL?

   A.   Change, service change, modification

   B.   Standard change, normal change, emergency change

   C.   User change, IT change, business change

   D.   Minor change, major change, urgent change

The three types of change defining by ITIL are standard change, normal change and emergency change.

A standard change is a type of change that is pre-authorized, low risk, relatively common and follows a procedure or work instruction.

A normal change is a type of change that is not an emergency change or standard change.

An emergency change is a type of change that must be implemented in a time-sensitive manner in order to prevent loss to the business.

Question ID: 168 / Topic: Service Transition Major Processes

31. Which of the following is the best description of the Service Desk function?

    A. ***The single point of contact for all operational issues from users***

    B. The single point of contact for all business changes

    C. The single point of contact for vendors to submit incidents

    D. The single point of contact between customers and IT

    The Service Desk serves as the single point of contact for all operational issues with users. The Service Desk restores services as quickly as possible through the Incident Management process as well as deals with requests from users through Request Fulfillment.

    Question ID: 302 / Topic: Major Functions (Service Desk)

32. To which of the following does the term service metric refer?

    A. ***The end-to-end measurement of a service***

    B. The measurement of customer satisfaction

    C. The response time at the Service Desk

    D. The measurement of the underlying processes that support the service

    The three types of metrics are technology (the underlying components), process (the service management processes that support the service) and service (the end-to-end measurements of the service).

    Question ID: 183 / Topic: Key Principles and Models

33. Which of the following is not a classification of a service?

    A. ***External service***

    B. Core service

    C. Enabling service

    D. Enhancing service

    Services can be classified as core, enabling and enhancing services.

    Question ID: 33 / Topic: Service Management as a Practice

34. For what is Application Management not responsible?

   A. Developing code required for applications

   B. Supporting applications

   C. Assisting with the design, testing and deployment of applications

   D. All of the above

Service Operation functions include the Service Desk, Application Management, Technical Management and IT Operation Management. Technical Management and Application Management are custodians of information with regard to their areas (infrastructure and applications) as well as provide resources to support the activities throughout the service lifecycle.

Application Management specifically is not responsible for the development of application code. This is the responsibility of Application Development.

Question ID: 313 / Topic: Minor Functions

35. Providing a consistent and single source of information for all services that are in operation or are prepared to be run operationally is the responsibility of which process?

   A. Service Strategy

   B. Service Level Management

   C. Service Catalog Management

   D. Service Operation

Providing a consistent and single source of information for all services that are in operation or are prepared to be run operationally is the responsibility Service Catalog Management.

Service Strategy and Service Operation are not processes.

Question ID: 271 / Topic: Service Design Minor Processes

36. To what does the statement "ensures that policies and strategy are actually implemented, and that required processes are correctly followed" refer?

    A. Assurance

    B. *Governance*

    C. Strategy

    D. Audit

Governance ensures that polices and strategy are actually implemented, and that required processes are correctly followed. Governance includes defining roles and responsibilities, measuring and reporting, and taking actions to resolve any issues identified. Governance can also be referred to as "ensuring fairness and transparency".

Question ID: 74 / Topic: Generic Concepts and Definitions

37. The measure of how long a service, component or CI can perform its agreed function without interruption refers to which of the following terms?

    A. Availability

    B. *Reliability*

    C. Maintainability

    D. Serviceability

Availability refers to the ability of a service, component or CI to perform its agreed function when required.

Reliability refers to a measure of how long a service, component or CI can perform its agreed function without interruption.

Maintainability refers to a measure of how quickly and effectively a service, component or CI can be restored to normal working after a failure.

Serviceability refers to the ability of a third-party supplier to meet the terms of its contract.

Question ID: 190 / Topic: Service Design Minor Processes

38. What is a Configuration Item (CI)?

    A. Business assets that support critical business processes

    B. Anything necessary in the delivery of technical services

    C. Any asset of an organization

    D. Anything that is under the control of Configuration Management

A Configuration Item (CI) is anything that is under the control of Configuration Management. CIs are any component, document, record, person, process, service, etc, that is used to provide a service.

Question ID: 164 / Topic: Service Transition Minor Processes

39. Which of the following does service automation improve?

    A. Capabilities and resources

    B. Functions and processes

    C. Utility and warranty

    D. Value and cost

Service automation is considered to improve the utility and warranty of services and underlying processes. Service automation improves consistency and reduces variation.

Question ID: 12 / Topic: Technology and Architecture

40. What is the purpose of IT Service Continuity Management?

    A. To support the overall Business Continuity Management process

    B. To monitor the availability of business processes

    C. To provide for disaster recovery of IT services

    D. To deliver plans for IT to support the business

IT Service Continuity Management supports the overall Business Continuity Management (BCM) process through the regular review of risks conducted in part through a BIA. Monitoring the availability of business processes is beyond the scope of IT Service Continuity Management.

Providing for IT service disaster recovery is too narrow of a scope and does not reflect the support for the business.

Question ID: 250 / Topic: Service Design Minor Processes

41. What are the three types of metrics as defined within CSI?

    A. Process, technology, service

    B. Program, Project and Personnel

    C. Organization, Business, Customer

    D. Baseline, benchmark, audit

The three types of metrics are technology (the underlying components), process (the service management processes that support the service) and service (the end-to-end measurements of the service).

Question ID: 181 / Topic: Key Principles and Models

42. In which stage of the service lifecycle include Service Catalog Management, Supplier Management and Information Security Management?

    A. Service Strategy

    B. Service Design

    C. Service Transition

    D. Service Operation

Service Design includes the processes of:

- Service Catalog Management
- Service Level Management
- Supplier Management
- Availability Management
- Capacity Management
- Information Security Management
- IT Service Continuity Management

Question ID: 247 / Topic: The ITIL Service Lifecycle

43. Which Service Operation function is responsible to be the custodian of information regarding the infrastructure?

    A.   Application Management

    B.   Facilities Management

    C.   Configuration Management

    D.   *Technical Management*

Service Operation functions include the Service Desk, Application Management, Technical Management and IT Operation Management. Technical Management and Application Management are custodians of information with regard to their areas (infrastructure and applications) as well as provide resources to support the activities throughout the service lifecycle.

Question ID: 314 / Topic: Minor Functions

44. Services facilitate what?

    A.   Risks

    B.   Revenue

    C.   *Outcomes*

    D.   Costs

A service is defined as a means of delivering value to customers by facilitating the outcomes customers want to achieve without the ownership of costs and risks.

Question ID: 28 / Topic: Service Management as a Practice

45. To what does the term 'rights' refer?

    A.   *The permissions granted to a user or role*

    B.   Information about a user that distinguishes one individual user from another

    C.   The level or extent of a service's functionality that a user is entitled to

    D.   None of the above

Identity is information about a user that distinguishes one individual user from another and is used to grant rights.

Rights refers to the permissions granted to a user or role.

Access refers to the level or extent of a service's functionality that a user is entitled to.

Question ID: 151 / Topic: Service Operation Minor Processes

46. Which of the following is the best description of IT Service Management?

    A. A means of delivering value to customers by facilitating outcomes customers want to achieve without the ownership of costs and risks

    B. **The implementation and management of quality IT services that meet the needs of the business**

    C. Both of the above

    D. None of the above

IT Service Management is defined as the implementation and management of quality IT services that meet the needs of the business. A means of delivering value to customers by facilitating outcomes customers want to achieve without the ownership of costs and risks is the definition of services.

Question ID: 39 / Topic: Service Management as a Practice

47. The main output of Service Operation is which of the following?

    A. Tested services to Continual Service Improvement

    B. Service Performance Reports to Service Design

    C. Service Operations Package to Service Transition

    D. **Service Performance Reports to Continual Service Improvement**

The service performance reports from operational services in Service Operation are inputs to Continual Service Improvement to identify opportunities for improvement.

Question ID: 298 / Topic: The ITIL Service Lifecycle

48. What is a customer-based Service Level Agreement (SLA)?

    A. An SLA between customers

    B. **An SLA for a single customer for all services for that customer**

    C. An SLA for a single service applicable to all customers of that service

    D. None of the above

A service-based SLA is an SLA for a single service applicable to all customers of that service.

A customer-based SLA is an SLA for a single customer for all services for that customer.

Question ID: 231 / Topic: Service Design Major Processes

49. The two sub-functions of IT Operation Management are which of the following?

    A.   Request Management and Data Center Management

    B.   Application Management and Technical Management

    C.   Operations Control and Facilities Management

    D.   Facilities Management and Request Management

Service Operation functions include the Service Desk, Application Management, Technical Management and IT Operation Management. Facilities Management and Operations Control are sub-functions of IT Operation Management.

Question ID: 311 / Topic: Minor Functions

50. To what does the term 'stakeholder' refer?

    A.   The customers who fund the service

    B.   The users who use a service

    C.   Anyone with an interest in an organization, project, service, etc.

    D.   The people performing the activities within a process

A stakeholder could include anyone involved or interested in the outcome of an organization, project, service in any way.

Question ID: 43 / Topic: Service Management as a Practice

51. What would be the next step in the Continual Service Improvement Model / Approach after

   1. What is the vision?

   2. Where are we now?

   3. Where do we want to be?

   4. How do we get there?

   5. Did we get there?

   A. How much did it cost?

   B. *How do we keep the momentum going?*

   C. What was the value on investment?

   D. What is the Total Cost of Ownership (TCO)?

The CSI Model / Approach outlines:
- What is the vision?
- Where are we now?
- Where do we want to be?
- How do we get there?
- Did we get there?
- How do we keep the momentum going?

Question ID: 222 / Topic: Key Principles and Models

52. Which stage of the service lifecycle is responsible for the design of new and changed services?

   A. Service Level Management

   B. Service Transition

   C. Service Strategy

   D. *Service Design*

Service Design is the stage of the lifecycle that is responsible for the design of new and changed services?

Service Level Management is not a stage of the service lifecycle.

Question ID: 264 / Topic: The ITIL Service Lifecycle

53. The purpose of Access Management is what?

    A. To define security policies to be followed

    B. To provide the right for users to be able to use a service or group of services

    C. To audit security throughout the service provider organization

    D. To ensure that access to services is available to all who ask

Access Management is the process of granting authorized users the right to use a service, while preventing access to non-authorized users. Access Management does not determine who has the right to use a service, but follows the policies defined in Service Design.

Question ID: 149 / Topic: Service Operation Minor Processes

54. Which of the following is not a value to business of the Service Strategy stage of the service lifecycle?

    A. Effectively design new and changed services

    B. Enable an understanding of what types and levels of services make its customer successful

    C. Enable the activities performed by the service provider to be linked to business outcomes enabling the service provider to be seen as contributing to the value of the business

    D. Facilitate functional and transparent communications between the customer and the service provider so that both have a consistent understanding of what is required and how it will be delivered

Service Design is responsible for the design of new and changed services. The remaining answers are a part of the value that Service Strategy provides to the business.

Question ID: 72 / Topic: The ITIL Service Lifecycle

55. Which of the following statements regarding Patterns of Business Activity is not correct?

    A. They are dynamic over time

    B. They represent the dynamics of the business

    C. They are impossible to forecast

    D. They should be documented and be an input to Capacity Management to plan capacity

Patterns of Business Activity (PBAs) represent the workload profiles of one or more business activities and represent the dynamics of the business.

Question ID: 100 / Topic: Service Strategy Minor Processes

56. Which of the following activities is carried out in the "Where do we want to be" step of the Continual Service Improvement model?

    A. Aligning the business and IT strategies

    B. Implementing service and process improvements

    C. Creating a baseline

    D. Defining measurable targets

The CSI Model / Approach outlines:

- What is the vision?
- Where are we now?
- Where do we want to be?
- How do we get there?
- Did we get there?
- How do we keep the momentum going?

Question ID: 221 / Topic: Key Principles and Models

57. Management, organization, processes and knowledge refer to what type of service asset?

    A. Functions

    B. Outcome support

    C. Resources

    D. Capabilities

This is an example of capabilities, the intangible component of service assets.

Question ID: 63 / Topic: Generic Concepts and Definitions

58. Which of the following statements regarding Problem Management are correct?

   1. When resolutions to problems require a change, they do not have to go through Change Management.

   2. Problem Management stores information about the underlying errors and workarounds in the Known Error Database (KEDB).

   3. Problem categorization and incident categorization are most likely to be identical.

   4. Problem Management activities are entirely reactive.

   A. 1, 3 and 4

   B. 2 only

   C. 4 only

   D. 2 and 3 only

All changes must go through Change Management. Problem Management includes reactive and proactive (such as trend analysis) activities.

Question ID: 145 / Topic: Service Operation Major Processes

59. What is a service-based Service Level Agreement (SLA)?

   A. An SLA between service providers

   B. An SLA for a single customer for all services for that customer

   C. An SLA for a single service applicable to all customers of that service

   D. An SLA between two parts of the same organization

A service-based SLA is an SLA for a single service applicable to all customers of that service.

A customer-based SLA is an SLA for a single customer for all services for that customer.

Question ID: 229 / Topic: Service Design Major Processes

60. What Service Operation process is responsible for managing the lifecycle of all service requests from the users?

   A. *Request Fulfillment*

   B. Request Management

   C. Service Desk

   D. Incident Management

Request Fulfillment is responsible for managing the lifecycle of all service requests from the users.

Question ID: 134 / Topic: Service Operation Minor Processes

61. Which of the following is Supplier Management responsible for?

   A. Operational Level Agreements (OLA)

   B. *Underpinning contracts (UC)*

   C. Service Level Requirements (SLR)

   D. Service Level Agreements (SLA)

Supplier Management is the process within Service Design that is responsible for underpinning contracts.

Question ID: 255 / Topic: Service Design Minor Processes

62. What is the name of the set of documents that serves as the main output of Service Design into Service Transition?

   A. Service Transition Package (STP)

   B. Service Operation Package (SOP)

   C. *Service Design Package (SDP)*

   D. Service Level Package (SLP)

The Service Design Package (SDP) is the set of documents that includes everything necessary for the build, test, implementation and deployment of a service into operation. The SDP is the output from Service Design into Service Transition.

Question ID: 300 / Topic: The ITIL Service Lifecycle

63. Which of the following characteristics do not contribute to the success of ITIL?

    A. ITIL is vendor-neutral

    B. ITIL is non-prescriptive

    C. ITIL is totally independent of any other standard, methodology or framework

    D. ITIL represents best practice

ITIL has achieved success because it is vendor-neutral, non-prescriptive, and represents the best practice learning experiences of best-in-class service providers.

Question ID: 26 / Topic: Service Management as a Practice

64. Which of the following is the best definition of a risk?

    A. A possible event that could cause harm or loss

    B. The discontinuation of a project

    C. The potential reorganization of the service provider

    D. The analysis of things that might happen to affect the service

A risk is defined as a possible event that could cause harm or loss. A potential reorganization could be a risk, but it is not inclusive of all risks that could be encountered.

Question ID: 96 / Topic: Generic Concepts and Definitions

65.   Which of the following is the best description of reliability?

   A.   The ability of a service, component or CI to perform its agreed function when required

   B.   *A measure of how long a service, component or CI can perform its agreed function without interruption*

   C.   A measure of how quickly and effectively a service, component or CI can be restored to normal working after a failure

   D.   The ability of a third-party supplier to meet the terms of its contract

Availability refers to the ability of a service, component or CI to perform its agreed function when required.

Reliability refers to a measure of how long a service, component or CI can perform its agreed function without interruption.

Maintainability refers to a measure of how quickly and effectively a service, component or CI can be restored to normal working after a failure.

Serviceability refers to the ability of a third-party supplier to meet the terms of its contract.

Question ID: 185 / Topic: Service Design Minor Processes

66.   A notification that a threshold has been violated is called what?

   A.   Event

   B.   Warning

   C.   *Alert*

   D.   Incident

An alert is a notification that a threshold has been reached, something has changed, or a failure has occurred.

Question ID: 123 / Topic: Service Operation Minor Processes

67. What are the first four steps of the CSI Model / CSI Approach?

    A. Identify measurable targets, understand the vision, outline the plan for improvement, assess the current environment

    B. Understand the vision, assess the current environment, identify measurable targets, outline a plan for improvement

    C. Assess the current environment, understand the vision, identify measurable targets, outline the plan for improvement

    D. Outline the plan for improvement, understand the vision, assess the current environment, identify measurable targets

The steps in the CSI Model / CSI Approach are:
- What is the vision?
- Where are we now?
- Where do we want to be?
- How do we get there?
- Did we get there?
- How do we keep the momentum going?

Question ID: 205 / Topic: Key Principles and Models

68. What is an underpinning contract (UC)?

    A. An agreement between two parts of the same organization

    B. An agreement between and IT service provider and an external third party

    C. A requirement for a specific aspect of an IT service

    D. An agreement between IT and their customer

Service Level Agreements are agreements between IT and their customer.

Operational Level Agreements are agreements between two parts of the same organization.

Underpinning contracts are agreements between and IT service provider and an external third party.

Service Level Requirements are requirements for a specific aspect of an IT service.

Question ID: 162 / Topic: Service Design Minor Processes

69. What is an Operational Level Agreement (OLA)?

   A. *An agreement between two parts of the same organization*

   B. An agreement between and IT service provider and an external third party

   C. A requirement for a specific aspect of an IT service

   D. An agreement between IT and their customer

Service Level Agreements are agreements between IT and their customer.

Operational Level Agreements are agreements between two parts of the same organization.

Underpinning contracts are agreements between and IT service provider and an external third party.

Service Level Requirements are requirements for a specific aspect of an IT service.

Question ID: 159 / Topic: Service Design Major Processes

70. To what does the phrase "those who buy goods or services" refer?

   A. *Customers*

   B. Users

   C. Service providers

   D. Suppliers

Customers are those who buy goods or services. The customer of an IT service provider is the person or group who defines and agrees to the service level targets.

Question ID: 104 / Topic: Generic Concepts and Definitions

71. Which of the following is not a type of event?

   A. Informational

   B. Warning

   C. Exception

   D. *Alert*

The types of events include informational, warning and exception

Question ID: 120 / Topic: Service Operation Minor Processes

72. Incident prioritization is determined by what?

   A.   Time and complexity

   B.   Resources and capabilities

   C.   Complexity and resources

   D.   Urgency and impact

The priority of an incident is determined by the impact (the level of disruption to the business) and urgency (how quickly the business needs a resolution).

Question ID: 126 / Topic: Service Operation Major Processes

73. Capabilities are which of the following:

   A.   The intangible elements of a service asset

   B.   The tangible elements of a service asset

   C.   The money the service asset requires to procure it

   D.   The value the service provider delivers to the business

Service assets are any resource or capability of a service provider. Resources are tangible. Capabilities are intangible.

Question ID: 59 / Topic: Generic Concepts and Definitions

74. To what does the phrase "any change of state that has significance for the management of a service" refer?

   A.   Event

   B.   Alert

   C.   Change

   D.   Service request

An event is defined as any change of state that has significance for the management of a configuration item or service.

Question ID: 118 / Topic: Service Operation Minor Processes

75. What is the last step in the CSI Model / CSI Approach?

    A. Establish a baseline

    B. Identify further opportunities for improvement

    C. Understand the vision for improvement

    D. Outline the plans for improvement

The steps in the CSI Model / CSI Approach are:
- What is the vision?
- Where are we now?
- Where do we want to be?
- How do we get there?
- Did we get there?
- How do we keep the momentum going?

Question ID: 204 / Topic: Key Principles and Models

76. Service metrics measure which of the following?

    A. Underlying components that support services

    B. Customer service statistics

    C. End-to-end service

    D. Resources and capabilities

Service metrics measure end-to-end services.

Question ID: 227 / Topic: Generic Concepts and Definitions

77. A measure of how quickly and effectively a service, component or CI can be restored to normal working after a failure refers to which of the following terms?

    A. Availability
    B. Reliability
    C. *Maintainability*
    D. Serviceability

Availability refers to the ability of a service, component or CI to perform its agreed function when required.

Reliability refers to a measure of how long a service, component or CI can perform its agreed function without interruption.

Maintainability refers to a measure of how quickly and effectively a service, component or CI can be restored to normal working after a failure.

Serviceability refers to the ability of a third-party supplier to meet the terms of its contract.

Question ID: 191 / Topic: Service Design Minor Processes

78. Complementary guidance refers to what?

    A. The free process maps that are included as available download
    B. The service that ITIL provides to assess a service provider's process maturity
    C. The industry that has been created around the service management profession
    D. *Additional publications providing guidance specific to industry sectors, organization types, operating models and technology architectures*

The complementary set of ITIL publications provide guidance in addition to the core volumes specific to industry sectors, organization types, operating models and technology architectures.

Question ID: 68 / Topic: The ITIL Service Lifecycle

79. Which of the following is the best description of a standard change?

   A.   A pre-authorized change with an accepted and established procedure

   B.   A change to the organizational policies and standards

   C.   A checklist for changes

   D.   A change that does not require following the Change Management process

A standard change is a type of change that is pre-authorized by Change Management and has an established procedure.

Question ID: 293 / Topic: Service Transition Major Processes

80. Which process is responsible for the negotiation of underpinning contracts?

   A.   Service Catalog Management

   B.   Supplier Management

   C.   Service Level Management

   D.   Contract Management

Supplier Management is the process within Service Design that is responsible for underpinning contracts.

Question ID: 254 / Topic: Service Design Minor Processes

81. Which of the following is not an advantage provided by service automation?

   A.   Increased consistency in reporting

   B.   Easier adjustment of workload to meet capacity demands

   C.   Improved consistency of service

   D.   Improved organizational structure

Service automation provides the following advantages:

   • Easier adjustment of capacity in response to variations in demand

   • Ability to handle capacity with fewer restrictions across time zones and after hours

   • Provides a good basis for measurement

   • Improved scheduling, routing and allocation of resources

   • Means for capturing knowledge

Question ID: 11 / Topic: Technology and Architecture

82. Which of the following statements regarding Business Relationship Management (BRM) and Service Level Management (SLM) is/are correct?

   1. BRM focuses on user satisfaction

   2. SLM focuses on strategic relationships

   3. SLM focuses on delivering specific levels of service to the business

   4. BRM focuses on delivering long-term customer satisfaction

    A.   None of the above

    B.   1, 2 and 3 only

    C.   3 and 4 only

    D.   All of the above

Business Relationship Management (BRM) focuses primarily on long-term customer satisfaction at the strategic and tactical levels while Service Level Management (SLM) focuses primarily on delivering specific levels of service at the operational and tactical levels.

Question ID: 241 / Topic: Service Design Major Processes

83. Which of the following would not be stored in the DML?

    A.   Change schedule for a business service

    B.   Video files as part of a service

    C.   Desktop images for standard desktop configurations

    D.   Application release candidates from the application development team

The DML is the storage location for definitive versions of all media assets including electronic and physical media CIs.

Question ID: 178 / Topic: Service Transition Minor Processes

84. Which Service Design process performs service reviews with the customer on a regular basis?

    A.   Service Operation

    B.   Service Catalog Management

    C.   Service Level Management

    D.   Service Reporting

Service Level Management build relationships with customers to understand their level of service to be provided. One of the Service Level Management activities is to perform service reviews on a regular basis with the customers.

Service Operation and Service Reporting are not processes within Service Design.

Question ID: 262 / Topic: Service Design Major Processes

85. Order the following Continual Service Improvement (CSI) implementation steps into the correct sequence in alignment with the Plan, Do, Check, Act (PDCA) model

    1. Allocate roles and responsibilities to work on CSI initiatives

    2. Measure and review that the CSI plan is executed and its objectives are being achieved

    3. Identify the scope, objectives and requirements for CSI

    4. Implement CSI enhancement

        A.   3-1-2-4

        B.   4-3-1-2

        C.   2-3-1-4

        D.   2-1-4-3

The following is the best match to the PDCA cycle:

PLAN: Identify the scope, objectives and requirements for CSI

DO: Allocate roles and responsibilities to work on CSI initiatives

CHECK: Measure and review that the CSI plan is executed and its objectives are being achieved

ACT: Implement CSI enhancements

Question ID: 223 / Topic: Key Principles and Models

86. Which of the following is not a function within Service Operation?

    A.   Application Management

    B.   Technical Management

    C.   Facilities Management

    D.   Request Fulfillment

Service Operation functions include the Service Desk, Application Management, Technical Management and IT Operation Management. Facilities Management and Operations Management are sub-functions of IT Operation Management.

Question ID: 310 / Topic: Major Functions (Service Desk)

87. Which of the following statements about Configuration Items (CIs) is/are true?

    1. Configuration Management monitors the performance characteristics of every CI

    2. CIs have attributes in which to record information about that CI or CI type

        A.   1 only

        B.   2 only

        C.   1 and 2

        D.   Neither statement is correct

Configuration Items (CIs) are anything under the control of Configuration Management. Configuration Management tracks the status of CIs through the life of the CI, but is not concerned with the performance characteristics of the CI. Other processes, such as Availability and Capacity Management are concerned with the performance of CIs.

Question ID: 165 / Topic: Service Transition Minor Processes

88. Which model provides a view of the services, assets and
     infrastructure and their relationships to each other?

     A. Change Model

     B. Incident Model

     C. *Configuration Model*

     D. Request Model

Service Asset and Configuration Management records the status of
CIs for a service. A configuration model is used to document the
relationships between assets, the services and infrastructure.

Question ID: 295 / Topic: Service Transition Minor Processes

89. The service lifecycle refers to all stages in the life of an IT
     service and includes the stages of Service Operation, Continual
     Service Improvement, Service Design and what other stage(s)?

     1. Service Optimization

     2. Service Definition

     3. Service Transition

     4. Service Outcomes

     5. Service Strategy

         A. 1 and 2 only

         B. 2, 3 and 5 only

         C. *3 and 5 only*

         D. 2, 3, 4 and 5 only

The service lifecycle refers to all stages in the life of an IT service
and includes service strategy, service design, service transition,
service operation and continual service improvement.

Question ID: 66 / Topic: The ITIL Service Lifecycle

90. What is the relationship between metrics and Key Performance Indicators (KPIs)?

   A. All metrics are KPIs

   B. They are the same thing

   C. *KPIs are the most important metrics that support CSFs*

   D. They are unrelated

CSFs are the things that must happen if an IT service, process, plan, project or other activity is to succeed. CSFs are measured through a small number of KPIs. KPIs are the most important and indicative metrics used to measure the achievement of CSFs.

Question ID: 208 / Topic: Key Principles and Models

91. What is referred to by the phrase "represents the commitments and investments made by a service provider across all customers and market spaces?"

   A. Service Strategy

   B. *Service Portfolio*

   C. Service Investment

   D. Service Value

The service portfolio represents the commitments and investments made by a service provider across all customer and market spaces. The service portfolio is the complete set of services that is managed by a service provider across the entire service lifecycle.

Question ID: 86 / Topic: Service Strategy Minor Processes

92. Which of the following techniques is most often used to assess risks to the business due to loss of IT service?

   A. Knowledge transfer

   B. RACI Model

   C. Component Failure Impact Analysis (CFIA)

   D. *Business Impact Analysis (BIA)*

The BIA is a technique used within IT Service Continuity Management (ITSCM) to assess the risk to the business due to loss of IT service.

Question ID: 253 / Topic: Service Design Minor Processes

93. What is the first step in the CSI Model / CSI Approach?

 A. ***What is the vision?***

 B. Where are we now?

 C. How do we get there?

 D. How do we keep the momentum going?

The steps in the CSI Model / CSI Approach are:
- What is the vision?
- Where are we now?
- Where do we want to be?
- How do we get there?
- Did we get there?
- How do we keep the momentum going?

Question ID: 202 / Topic: Key Principles and Models

94. Which stage of the Service Lifecycle includes the processes of Availability Management and Supplier Management?

 A. Service Strategy

 B. ***Service Design***

 C. Service Transition

 D. Service Operation

Service Design includes the processes of:
- Service Catalog Management
- Service Level Management
- Supplier Management
- Availability Management
- Capacity Management
- Information Security Management
- IT Service Continuity Management

Question ID: 248 / Topic: The ITIL Service Lifecycle

95. Which of the following responsibilities would be expected of a service owner?

    A.   Defining the process strategy

    B.   Carrying out the activities of a process

    C.   *Representing the service across the organization*

    D.   Implementing changes to a service

    The service owner represents a service across the organization. The service owner participates in service review meetings, CAB meetings as well as identifying opportunities for improvement.

    Question ID: 14 / Topic: Roles

96. What should the CSI register be part of?

    A.   CMS

    B.   *SKMS*

    C.   KEDB

    D.   DIKW Model

    The CSI register is a database or structured document used to record and manage improvement opportunities throughout their lifecycle. The CSI register is part of the Service Knowledge Management System (SKMS).

    Question ID: 219 / Topic: Generic Concepts and Definitions

97. Identifying ways to improve processes, services and become more cost effective is part of which stage of the service lifecycle?

    A.   Service Transition

    B.   Service Strategy

    C.   Service Operation

    D.   *Continual Service Improvement*

    Continual Service Improvement provides guidance on improving processes, services and providing more cost effective services without sacrificing customer satisfaction.

    Question ID: 225 / Topic: The ITIL Service Lifecycle

98. Which of the following would be the best example of an enabling service?

    A.   Shipping service that supports the business outcome of shipping products in a timely manner.

    B.   ***Network service that supports communication between components***

    C.   Service Desk

    D.   None of the above

Enabling services are those services that must be in place for the core service to operate effectively. In this case, the network service is the best example of an enabling service.

Question ID: 81 / Topic: Generic Concepts and Definitions

99. In which stage of the service lifecycle are the functional requirements documented and service levels agreed?

    A.   Service Strategy

    B.   Service Transition

    C.   ***Service Design***

    D.   Service Operation

Service Design is responsible for the documentation functional, operational, transition, and other requirements as well as determining the level of service to be provided and agreed to.

Question ID: 265 / Topic: The ITIL Service Lifecycle

100. What is an alert?

    A.   ***A notification that a threshold has been violated***

    B.   An occurrence that is significant for the management of a service

    C.   An audible notification

    D.   An emergency meeting to evaluate a change

An alert is a notification that a threshold has been reached, a failure has occurred, or something has changed.

Question ID: 122 / Topic: Service Operation Minor Processes

Sample Exam

Instructions

1. All 40 questions should be attempted

2. There are no trick questions

3. You have 60 minutes for this paper

4. You must get 26 or more correct to pass

1. Complementary guidance refers to what?

    A. The free process maps that are included as available download

    B. The service that ITIL provides to assess a service provider's process maturity

    C. The industry that has been created around the service management profession

    D. Additional publications providing guidance specific to industry sectors, organization types, operating models and technology architectures

2. What is a problem model?

    A. A way to resolve an incident in a standardized way

    B. A set of predefined steps to take when dealing with a particular type of problem

    C. A graphical representation of the cause of a problem

    D. A way to resolve all problems easily

3. To what does governance refer?

    A. A structured approach for continual optimization

    B. The actual audit of an organization

    C. Following the rules of the service provider

    D. Ensuring fairness and transparency

4. Which of the following statements about patterns of business activities are correct?

    A. Patterns of business activity cannot be predicted

    B. Patterns of business activity are always constant over time

    C. Patterns of business activity represent the dynamics of the business

    D. Patterns of business activity are only determined by the service provider

5. The set of tools and databases used to store a service provider's configuration information is called what?

    A. Configuration Management System

    B. Configuration Management Database

    C. Service Knowledge Management System

    D. Availability Management Information System

6. Within service management, organizational capabilities refer to what?

    A. Resources and capabilities

    B. Risks and costs

    C. Organization and management

    D. Processes and functions

7. The purpose of Change Management is which of the following?

    A. Control the performance of all service components and ensure that their relationships are documented

    B. Implement changes into the production environment through scheduled releases

    C. Control the lifecycle of all change, enabling beneficial changes to be made with minimum disruption to IT services

    D. All of the above

8. Which of the following is a hierarchy that is used in Knowledge Management?

    A. Information->Data->Wisdom->Knowledge

    B. Data->Knowledge->Wisdom->Information

    C. Wisdom->Knowledge->Information->Data

    D. Data->Information->Knowledge->Wisdom

9. What is an Operational Level Agreement (OLA)?

    A. An agreement between two parts of the same organization

    B. An agreement between and IT service provider and an external third party

    C. A requirement for a specific aspect of an IT service

    D. An agreement between IT and their customer

10. Which Service Operation function is responsible to be the custodian of knowledge related to the applications?

    A. Application Management

    B. Technical Management

    C. Configuration Management

    D. Service Desk

11. Which of the following is the best description of a Service Level Requirement (SLR)?

    A. A customer requirement for an aspect of a service

    B. A user requirement for an aspect of a service

    C. SLRs are the same as Service Acceptance Criteria (SAC)

    D. A target to be measured within an OLA

12. Within the RACI Model, 'Consulted' refers to what?

    A. The roles in charge of the process

    B. Two-way communication between stakeholders in a process or activity

    C. An agreement between the service provider and an external services organization

    D. One-way communication to keep others up to date on progress

13. Which of the following is the best description of the Service Desk function?

    A. The single point of contact for all operational issues from users

    B. The single point of contact for all business changes

    C. The single point of contact for vendors to submit incidents

    D. The single point of contact between customers and IT

14. Which of the following is not a type of event?

    A. Informational

    B. Warning

    C. Exception

    D. Alert

15. What is the best description of a service provider?

    A. An organization that meets all of the needs of their customer

    B. An organization that supports IT

    C. An organization that provides services to one or more internal or external customers

    D. An organization that IT provides that is in the service industry

16. Which of the following statements regarding value creation is incorrect?

    A. Value is always defined in terms of business outcomes

    B. Value is subjective

    C. Value is always defined in financial terms

    D. Customers play an important part in value determination

17. A business case can be described as what?

    A. A storage location for business files

    B. The financial analysis for a service management tool

    C. A decision support and planning tool

    D. None of the above

18. All services facilitate what?

    A. Risks

    B. Revenue

    C. Outcomes

    D. Costs

19. In which stage of the service lifecycle are the functional requirements documented and service levels agreed?

    A. Service Strategy

    B. Service Transition

    C. Service Design

    D. Service Operation

20. Reducing or eliminating the impact of an incident or problem for which a full resolution is not yet available is a description of which of the following terms?

    A. Workaround

    B. Resolution

    C. Incident

    D. Problem

21. Which of the following is not a value of Service Design?

    A. Reduced total cost of ownership

    B. Reduced funding of services

    C. Improved consistency of service

    D. Improved quality of service

22. A Business Impact Analysis (BIA) is part of which Service Design process?

   A. Financial Management

   B. Availability Management

   C. IT Service Continuity Management

   D. Disaster Recovery

23. Which of the following is a process within Service Transition?

   A. Capacity Management

   B. Problem Management

   C. Service Portfolio Management

   D. Knowledge Management

24. Which of the following is the best definition of a risk?

   A. A possible event that could cause harm or loss

   B. The discontinuation of a project

   C. The potential reorganization of the service provider

   D. The analysis of things that might happen to affect the service

25. Which of the following are within the scope of Service Strategy?

   1. Defining a strategy whereby a service provider will deliver services to meet a customer's business outcomes

   2. Defining a strategy for how to manage those services

   3. Defining a strategy to improve business revenue

      A. 1 only

      B. 2 only

      C. 3 only

      D. 1 and 2 only

26. A service does exactly what the users and customer require, but experiences severe outages. This is an example of what?

    A. High utility and high warranty

    B. High utility and low warranty

    C. Low utility and high warranty

    D. Low utility and low warranty

27. Which of the following are included in the five major aspects of design?

    1. Service solution itself

    2. Service operation process designs to support a new or changed service

    3. Technical architectures

    4. Environmental architectures

    5. Service Portfolio

        A. 1 and 2 only

        B. 2, 3 and 4 only

        C. None of these are included in the five major aspects of design

        D. All of the above

28. Specifically, which of the following does outcome refer to?

    A. Intended and actual results

    B. Resources and capabilities

    C. Processes and functions

    D. Utility and warranty

29. Other than the number of users impacted, what other factors can also contribute to the impact of an incident?

   1. Risk to life or limb

   2. Number of services affected

   3. Level of financial loss

   4. Effect on business reputation

   5. Regulatory or legislative breaches

      A.   2 only

      B.   All except 1

      C.   None of the above

      D.   All of the above

30. Warranty is the assurance that a service is fit for use. How else can warranty be expressed?

   A. Any means by which the service provider supports the service

   B. Any means by which the service is supported by an external third party guarantee

   C. Any means by which an organization that supports a service is defined

   D. Any means by which utility is made available to users

31. A type of Service Level Agreement (SLA) for a single service for all customers of that service is called what?

   A. Service-based SLA

   B. Customer-based SLA

   C. Single Service Agreement (SSA)

   D. Service Catalog

32. Which of the following activities is carried out in the "Where do we want to be" step of the Continual Service Improvement model?

   A. Aligning the business and IT strategies

   B. Implementing service and process improvements

   C. Creating a baseline

   D. Defining measurable targets

33. Capacity Management includes all of the following subprocesses except which?

    A. Service Capacity Management

    B. Customer Capacity Management

    C. Business Capacity Management

    D. Component Capacity Management

34. Which of the following is not a part of Supplier Management?

    A. Obtain value for money from suppliers

    B. Ensure that all contracts and agreements with suppliers support the needs of the business

    C. Ensure that suppliers meet their contractual commitments

    D. Ensure that Service Level Agreements are in place to support the business

35. The Service Design Package (SDP) is the output of which stage of the service lifecycle into which stage of the service lifecycle?

    A. Service Design to Service Operation

    B. Service Design to Service Transition

    C. Service Design to Continual Service Improvement

    D. Service Design to Service Strategy

36. Which of the following is not a part of the service portfolio?

    A. Service pipeline

    B. Service definition

    C. Service catalog

    D. Retired services

37. The Deming Cycle promotes which type of improvement?

    A. One-off improvements

    B. Ad-hoc improvements

    C. Steady, ongoing improvements

    D. Quick wins

38. Which of the following is the best description of urgency?

 A. The level of disruption to the business

 B. An emergency that needs to be handled in a timely manner

 C. How quickly the business needs a resolution

 D. The priority code of an incident

39. Which of the following is not an advantage provided by service automation?

 A. Increased consistency in reporting

 B. Easier adjustment of workload to meet capacity demands

 C. Improved consistency of service

 D. Improved organizational structure

40. To what does the term service asset refer?

 A. Any capability or resource of a service provider

 B. The resources that a service provider uses in the provisioning of services

 C. The skills and abilities of the people in the service provider organization

 D. The abilities of the business to achieve their desired outcomes

SAMPLE EXAM ANSWERS AND RATIONALES

Q#		Q#	
1	D	21	B
2	B	22	C
3	D	23	D
4	C	24	A
5	A	25	D
6	D	26	B
7	C	27	D
8	D	28	A
9	A	29	D
10	A	30	D
11	A	31	A
12	B	32	D
13	A	33	B
14	D	34	D
15	C	35	B
16	C	36	B
17	C	37	C
18	C	38	C
19	C	39	D
20	A	40	A

1. Complementary guidance refers to what?

    A. The free process maps that are included as available download

    B. The service that ITIL provides to assess a service provider's process maturity

    C. The industry that has been created around the service management profession

    D. ***Additional publications providing guidance specific to industry sectors, organization types, operating models and technology architectures***

The complementary set of ITIL publications provide guidance in addition to the core volumes specific to industry sectors, organization types, operating models and technology architectures.

Question ID: 68 / Topic: The ITIL Service Lifecycle

2. What is a problem model?

    A. A way to resolve an incident in a standardized way

    B. ***A set of predefined steps to take when dealing with a particular type of problem***

    C. A graphical representation of the cause of a problem

    D. A way to resolve all problems easily

A problem model is a set of predefined steps to take when dealing with a known type of problem. A problem model should include:

- The steps to take
- The chronological order to take these steps
- Responsibilities
- Timescales and thresholds
- Escalation procedures

Question ID: 131 / Topic: Service Operation Major Processes

3. To what does governance refer?

    A. A structured approach for continual optimization

    B. The actual audit of an organization

    C. Following the rules of the service provider

    D. Ensuring fairness and transparency

Governance ensures that polices and strategy are actually implemented, and that required processes are correctly followed. Governance includes defining roles and responsibilities, measuring and reporting, and taking actions to resolve any issues identified. Governance can also be referred to as "ensuring fairness and transparency".

Question ID: 75 / Topic: Generic Concepts and Definitions

4. Which of the following statements about patterns of business activities are correct?

    A. Patterns of business activity cannot be predicted

    B. Patterns of business activity are always constant over time

    C. Patterns of business activity represent the dynamics of the business

    D. Patterns of business activity are only determined by the service provider

Patterns of Business Activity (PBAs) represent the workload profiles of one or more business activities and represent the dynamics of the business.

Question ID: 99 / Topic: Service Strategy Minor Processes

5. The set of tools and databases used to store a service provider's configuration information is called what?

    A. Configuration Management System

    B. Configuration Management Database

    C. Service Knowledge Management System

    D. Availability Management Information System

The Configuration Management System (CMS) is the set of tools and databases used to store a service providers configuration information.

Question ID: 267 / Topic: Service Transition Minor Processes

6. Within service management, organizational capabilities refer to what?

    A. Resources and capabilities

    B. Risks and costs

    C. Organization and management

    D. Processes and functions

Service management is defined as a set of organizational capabilities for providing value to customers in the form of services. The organizational capabilities consist of the processes and functions within the service provider.

Question ID: 36 / Topic: Service Management as a Practice

7. The purpose of Change Management is which of the following?

    A. Control the performance of all service components and ensure that their relationships are documented

    B. Implement changes into the production environment through scheduled releases

    C. Control the lifecycle of all change, enabling beneficial changes to be made with minimum disruption to IT services

    D. All of the above

Change Management manages changes through their life. Changes are deployed into production through the Release and Deployment process. Change Management works closely with Service Asset and Configuration Management to track the configuration items affected by a change.

Question ID: 284 / Topic: Service Transition Major Processes

8. Which of the following is a hierarchy that is used in Knowledge Management?

    A. Information->Data->Wisdom->Knowledge

    B. Data->Knowledge->Wisdom->Information

    C. Wisdom->Knowledge->Information->Data

    D. Data->Information->Knowledge->Wisdom

The Knowledge Spiral, also known as the DIKW model in Knowledge Management stands for Data->Information->Knowledge->Wisdom.

Question ID: 297 / Topic: Service Transition Minor Processes

9. What is an Operational Level Agreement (OLA)?

   A. ***An agreement between two parts of the same organization***

   B. An agreement between and IT service provider and an external third party

   C. A requirement for a specific aspect of an IT service

   D. An agreement between IT and their customer

Service Level Agreements are agreements between IT and their customer.

Operational Level Agreements are agreements between two parts of the same organization.

Underpinning contracts are agreements between and IT service provider and an external third party.

Service Level Requirements are requirements for a specific aspect of an IT service.

Question ID: 159 / Topic: Service Design Major Processes

10. Which Service Operation function is responsible to be the custodian of knowledge related to the applications?

    A. ***Application Management***

    B. Technical Management

    C. Configuration Management

    D. Service Desk

Service Operation functions include the Service Desk, Application Management, Technical Management and IT Operation Management. Technical Management and Application Management are custodians of information with regard to their areas (infrastructure and applications) as well as provide resources to support the activities throughout the service lifecycle.

Question ID: 315 / Topic: Minor Functions

11. Which of the following is the best description of a Service Level Requirement (SLR)?

  A. A customer requirement for an aspect of a service

  B. A user requirement for an aspect of a service

  C. SLRs are the same as Service Acceptance Criteria (SAC)

  D. A target to be measured within an OLA

An SLR is defined as a customer requirement for an aspect of a service. SLRs are supported by Service Level Targets (SLTs) and documented within the Service Level Agreements (SLAs).

Question ID: 237 / Topic: Service Design Major Processes

12. Within the RACI Model, 'Consulted' refers to what?

  A. The roles in charge of the process

  B. Two-way communication between stakeholders in a process or activity

  C. An agreement between the service provider and an external services organization

  D. One-way communication to keep others up to date on progress

RACI stands for Responsible, Accountable, Consulted and Informed.

Responsible refers to the person or people responsible for correct execution.

Accountable refers to the person who has ownership of quality and the end result.

Consulted refers to the people who are consulted and whose opinions are sought.

Informed refers to the people who are kept up to date on progress.

Question ID: 6 / Topic: Roles

13. Which of the following is the best description of the Service Desk function?

   A. The single point of contact for all operational issues from users

   B. The single point of contact for all business changes

   C. The single point of contact for vendors to submit incidents

   D. The single point of contact between customers and IT

The Service Desk serves as the single point of contact for all operational issues with users. The Service Desk restores services as quickly as possible through the Incident Management process as well as deals with requests from users through Request Fulfillment.

Question ID: 302 / Topic: Major Functions (Service Desk)

14. Which of the following is not a type of event?

   A. Informational

   B. Warning

   C. Exception

   D. Alert

The types of events include informational, warning and exception

Question ID: 120 / Topic: Service Operation Minor Processes

15. What is the best description of a service provider?

   A. An organization that meets all of the needs of their customer

   B. An organization that supports IT

   C. An organization that provides services to one or more internal or external customers

   D. An organization that IT provides that is in the service industry

A service provider is defined as an organization supplying services to one or more internal or external customers.

Question ID: 37 / Topic: Service Management as a Practice

16. Which of the following statements regarding value creation is incorrect?

    A. Value is always defined in terms of business outcomes

    B. Value is subjective

    C. *Value is always defined in financial terms*

    D. Customers play an important part in value determination

Value is determined by the customer's perspective and is defined in terms of the business outcomes achieved, the customer's preferences and the customer's perceptions.

Question ID: 105 / Topic: Key Principles and Models

17. A business case can be described as what?

    A. A storage location for business files

    B. The financial analysis for a service management tool

    C. *A decision support and planning tool*

    D. None of the above

A business case is a decision support and planning tool that projects the likely consequences of a business action.

Question ID: 91 / Topic: Service Strategy Minor Processes

18. All services facilitate what?

    A. Risks

    B. Revenue

    C. *Outcomes*

    D. Costs

A service is defined as a means of delivering value to customers by facilitating the outcomes customers want to achieve without the ownership of costs and risks.

Question ID: 28 / Topic: Service Management as a Practice

19. In which stage of the service lifecycle are the functional requirements documented and service levels agreed?

    A. Service Strategy

    B. Service Transition

    C. *Service Design*

    D. Service Operation

    Service Design is responsible for the documentation functional, operational, transition, and other requirements as well as determining the level of service to be provided and agreed to.

    Question ID: 265 / Topic: The ITIL Service Lifecycle

20. Reducing or eliminating the impact of an incident or problem for which a full resolution is not yet available is a description of which of the following terms?

    A. *Workaround*

    B. Resolution

    C. Incident

    D. Problem

    A workaround is defined as reducing or eliminating the impact of an incident or problem for which a full resolution is not yet available.

    Question ID: 194 / Topic: Service Operation Major Processes

21. Which of the following is not a value of Service Design?

    A. Reduced total cost of ownership

    B. Reduced funding of services

    C. Improved consistency of service

    D. Improved quality of service

The values of Service Design as documented in ITIL include:

- Reduced total cost of ownership
- Improved quality of service
- Improved consistency of service
- Eased implementation of new or changed services
- Improved service alignment
- Improved service performance
- Improved IT governance
- Improved effectiveness of service management
- Improved information and decision-making
- Improved alignment with customer value and strategies

Question ID: 266 / Topic: The ITIL Service Lifecycle

22. A Business Impact Analysis (BIA) is part of which Service Design process?

    A. Financial Management

    B. Availability Management

    C. IT Service Continuity Management

    D. Disaster Recovery

The BIA is conducted as part of IT Service Continuity Management (ITSCM). Financial Management is not a Service Design process, but is included in Service Strategy. The BIA can be used to support Availability Management, but it is not part of the Availability Management process. Disaster Recovery is not a process recognized by ITIL.

Question ID: 252 / Topic: Service Design Minor Processes

23. Which of the following is a process within Service Transition?

    A. Capacity Management

    B. Problem Management

    C. Service Portfolio Management

    D. *Knowledge Management*

Service Transition includes the processes of:

- Change Management

- Service Asset and Configuration Management

- Release and Deployment Management

- Knowledge Management

- Transition Planning and Support

Question ID: 296 / Topic: Service Transition Minor Processes

24. Which of the following is the best definition of a risk?

    A. *A possible event that could cause harm or loss*

    B. The discontinuation of a project

    C. The potential reorganization of the service provider

    D. The analysis of things that might happen to affect the service

A risk is defined as a possible event that could cause harm or loss. A potential reorganization could be a risk, but it is not inclusive of all risks that could be encountered.

Question ID: 96 / Topic: Generic Concepts and Definitions

25. Which of the following are within the scope of Service Strategy?

    1. Defining a strategy whereby a service provider will deliver services to meet a customer's business outcomes

    2. Defining a strategy for how to manage those services

    3. Defining a strategy to improve business revenue

    A. 1 only

    B. 2 only

    C. 3 only

    D. *1 and 2 only*

Defining business strategy are beyond the scope of the IT service provider and therefore beyond the scope of Service Strategy.

Question ID: 73 / Topic: The ITIL Service Lifecycle

26. A service does exactly what the users and customer require, but experiences severe outages. This is an example of what?

    A. High utility and high warranty

    B. *High utility and low warranty*

    C. Low utility and high warranty

    D. Low utility and low warranty

Utility refers to what a service does. In this case, utility is high because it does what the customers and users need. Warranty is the assurance that a product or service will meet its intended requirements and is provided through availability, capacity, continuity and security. In this case is the warranty is low due to lack of availability.

Question ID: 48 / Topic: Generic Concepts and Definitions

27. Which of the following are included in the five major aspects of design?

    1. Service solution itself

    2. Service operation process designs to support a new or changed service

    3. Technical architectures

    4. Environmental architectures

    5. Service Portfolio

        A. 1 and 2 only

        B. 2, 3 and 4 only

        C. None of these are included in the five major aspects of design

        D. All of the above

The five major aspects of design are STAMP:

- Service solution
- Tools and technology (such as the service portfolio)
- Architectures
- Measurements and metrics
- Processes

(Remember STAMP)

Question ID: 220 / Topic: Key Principles and Models

28. Specifically, which of the following does outcome refer to?

    A. Intended and actual results

    B. Resources and capabilities

    C. Processes and functions

    D. Utility and warranty

Outcome is defined as the result of carrying out an activity, following a process, or delivering an IT service etc. The term is used to refer to intended results, as well as to actual results.

Question ID: 84 / Topic: Generic Concepts and Definitions

29. Other than the number of users impacted, what other factors can also contribute to the impact of an incident?

    1. Risk to life or limb

    2. Number of services affected

    3. Level of financial loss

    4. Effect on business reputation

    5. Regulatory or legislative breaches

        A. 2 only

        B. All except 1

        C. None of the above

        D. *All of the above*

The impact of an incident can be determined by financial and non-financial measures. All of these may contribute to the impact of an incident, problem, or change.

Question ID: 129 / Topic: Service Operation Major Processes

30. Warranty is the assurance that a service is fit for use. How else can warranty be expressed?

    A. Any means by which the service provider supports the service

    B. Any means by which the service is supported by an external third party guarantee

    C. Any means by which an organization that supports a service is defined

    D. *Any means by which utility is made available to users*

Warranty refers to the availability, capacity, continuity and security of a service and involves any means by which the utility of a service is made available to users.

Question ID: 49 / Topic: Generic Concepts and Definitions

31. A type of Service Level Agreement (SLA) for a single service for all customers of that service is called what?

    A. Service-based SLA

    B. Customer-based SLA

    C. Single Service Agreement (SSA)

    D. Service Catalog

A service-based SLA is an SLA for a single service applicable to all customers of that service.

A customer-based SLA is an SLA for a single customer for all services for that customer.

               Question ID: 230 / Topic: Service Design Major Processes

32. Which of the following activities is carried out in the "Where do we want to be" step of the Continual Service Improvement model?

    A. Aligning the business and IT strategies

    B. Implementing service and process improvements

    C. Creating a baseline

    D. Defining measurable targets

The CSI Model / Approach outlines:

- What is the vision?
- Where are we now?
- Where do we want to be?
- How do we get there?
- Did we get there?
- How do we keep the momentum going?

               Question ID: 221 / Topic: Key Principles and Models

33. Capacity Management includes all of the following subprocesses except which?

    A. Service Capacity Management

    B. *Customer Capacity Management*

    C. Business Capacity Management

    D. Component Capacity Management

Capacity Management includes the subprocesses of Business Capacity Management, Service Capacity Management and Component Capacity Management.

Question ID: 244 / Topic: Service Design Minor Processes

34. Which of the following is not a part of Supplier Management?

    A. Obtain value for money from suppliers

    B. Ensure that all contracts and agreements with suppliers support the needs of the business

    C. Ensure that suppliers meet their contractual commitments

    D. *Ensure that Service Level Agreements are in place to support the business*

The overall purpose of Supplier Management is to obtain value for money from suppliers and to provide seamless quality of IT service to the business by ensuring that all contracts and agreements with suppliers support the needs of the business and that all suppliers meet their contractual commitments.

Question ID: 256 / Topic: Service Design Minor Processes

35. The Service Design Package (SDP) is the output of which stage of the service lifecycle into which stage of the service lifecycle?

    A. Service Design to Service Operation

    B. *Service Design to Service Transition*

    C. Service Design to Continual Service Improvement

    D. Service Design to Service Strategy

The Service Design Package (SDP) is the set of documents that includes everything necessary for the build, test, implementation and deployment of a service into operation. The SDP is the output from Service Design into Service Transition.

Question ID: 301 / Topic: The ITIL Service Lifecycle

36. Which of the following is not a part of the service portfolio?

   A. Service pipeline

   B. Service definition

   C. Service catalog

   D. Retired services

   The service portfolio contains the service pipeline, service catalog, and retired services.

   Question ID: 88 / Topic: Service Strategy Minor Processes

37. The Deming Cycle promotes which type of improvement?

   A. One-off improvements

   B. Ad-hoc improvements

   C. Steady, ongoing improvements

   D. Quick wins

   The Deming Cycle (Plan-Do-Check-Act) promotes steady, ongoing improvements.

   Question ID: 226 / Topic: Key Principles and Models

38. Which of the following is the best description of urgency?

   A. The level of disruption to the business

   B. An emergency that needs to be handled in a timely manner

   C. How quickly the business needs a resolution

   D. The priority code of an incident

   The priority of an incident is determined by the impact (the level of disruption to the business) and urgency (how quickly the business needs a resolution).

   Question ID: 127 / Topic: Service Operation Major Processes

39. Which of the following is not an advantage provided by service automation?

    A. Increased consistency in reporting

    B. Easier adjustment of workload to meet capacity demands

    C. Improved consistency of service

    D. *Improved organizational structure*

Service automation provides the following advantages:

- Easier adjustment of capacity in response to variations in demand
- Ability to handle capacity with fewer restrictions across time zones and after hours
- Provides a good basis for measurement
- Improved scheduling, routing and allocation of resources
- Means for capturing knowledge

Question ID: 11 / Topic: Technology and Architecture

40. To what does the term service asset refer?

    A. Any capability or resource of a service provider

    B. The resources that a service provider uses in the provisioning of services

    C. The skills and abilities of the people in the service provider organization

    D. The abilities of the business to achieve their desired outcomes

A service asset is defined as any resource or capability used by a service provider to deliver services to a customer.

Question ID: 57 / Topic: Generic Concepts and Definitions

69690364R00062

Made in the USA
San Bernardino, CA
19 February 2018